3 – Villa Buzzati, Traverso
Visome, San Pellegrino

This is a Romantic complex which is situated in a beautiful panoramic area which looks out over Belluno and the local Alps, above the Piave river. The residential building is made up of a central body with frescoes by Vizzotto, and a neo-Gothic east wing by Andrea Sala with frescoes by Pompeo Molmenti and Pavolin; the façade contains paintings by Luigi da Rios. A faux ruined castle faces the villa from the garden.

There is also a small, decagonal church erected after 1530 by Jacopo Sacello, member of the family who originally owned by the building, where the writer Dino Buzzati, a one-time resident of the villa, is buried.

Veneto Villas

i piccoli
di arsenale

Valeria Bové

Veneto Villas

arsenale editrice

Valeria Bové
VENETO VILLAS

photography
Mark E. Smith

layout
Stefano Grandi

print
EBS Editoriale Bortolazzi-Stei
Verona

first edition
February 1999

Arsenale Editrice srl
San Polo 1789
I - 30125 Venice
Italy

Arsenale Editrice © 1998

ISBN 88-7743-203-9

Contents

Introduction

James Ackerman, the great commentator on architectural themes, generically defines the villa as a building that has been planned to satisfy its owner's desire for rest and leisure. Even though it might constitute the central element in some agricultural concern or other, the pleasurable element cannot be distinguished from its more pragmatic *raison d'être*, thus underlining the satisfying of psychological and ideological demands as opposed to material demands. The villa's basic programme has therefore remained substantially identical to the original one established by ancient Roman patricians.

It is impossible to understand the villa without taking into account its relationship with the city. That is, the villa exists not so much because it absolves autonomous functions, but rather as a counterbalance to the values and advantages offered by urban life – its economic status can thus be seen as complementary. It should be thought of as both an architectural and ideological paradigm, the significance of which is rooted in the contrast between country and city, where the virtues and pleasures of the former are antithetical to the vices and excesses of the latter. This ideological structure was broadly developed in Latin literature and surfaced again in later periods. The advantages and pleasures of villa life seem to have remained identical throughout the centuries: the practical benefits of country life, the health of the body assured thanks to fresh air and physical activity (especially hunting), rest and relaxation enhanced by reading and conversation with "virtuous" friends, and the contemplation of pleasant countryside views.

From an economic point of view, villas can be classified according to two types: a self-sufficient agricultural estate which also produces profits thanks to the commercialisation of its excess product; the villa described by Leon Battista Alberti as a residence conceived quite simply to delight, a place to which owners can retire from the world and seek repose. The latter type, for its construction and maintenance, obviously requires the use of excess funds deriving from the urban professions of its proprietors.

The villa is the expression of a complex of myths which are at the forefront of its realisation: an attraction for nature, the dialectics of the natural versus the artificial, the prerogative of privilege and power. Again, according to Ackerman the mythical nature of the ideology of the villa frees it from the material restrictions of use and productivity, and makes it ideally appropriate for the creative aspirations of its commissioners and artists.

Particularly in the Veneto, two principle themes emerge from an analysis of the villa: the problem of how the country is "used" by the urban nobility, expropriated of its power because of the advance in Venice's power; the representation, from about the mid 15th century, in humanistic writings, of a space dedicated to *otium*, intended as a flight from reality, and justified through recourse to ancient precedent.

Architecturally, the first examples of noble homes in the Veneto are rural buildings designed for desultory trips into the country by the owners. It is in the early 15th century, when Venice annexed Vicenza in 1404 and then Padua and Verona in 1405, that the "Venetian villa" can really be thought of as a distinct architectural category. Various reasons have been given for Venice's political and economic development: the sudden availability of large tracts of land, the difficulties faced by maritime commerce due to the changes in sea routes following Portugal's discovery of new lands and the Turks' conquest of Constantinople, as well as the increase in agricultural prices in the early 16th century. But above all there was a change in mentality; the idea of the "merchant" and "market" acquired different meanings. The traditionally mercantile dominant class in the Veneto seems to have followed a trend set by the nobles of the dominant city. That is, this new class, which was still strictly linked to a feudal past, saw in the re-population and empowering of the countryside a legitimate means of reacting against the Republic's annexing of their cities, which had effectively weakened their real control over the cities themselves.

A few hypotheses have been put forward regarding the genesis of the typology of the villa in the Veneto territory. One sees the constitution of the model in a type deriving from the concept of the castle, which, once it had lost its predominantly defensive role and function, was transformed into a residence for free time and repose. Another prototype, nonetheless deriving from fortified buildings, is the loggia-ed villa, that is a portico along the ground floor and a loggia along the first, very often flanking a massive vertical body which was reminiscent of ancient tower structures. However, many villas of the 15th century, and not only, derive from the prototype of the Venetian *palazzo*. Palladio's villa-temple type, and the two-storey villa-*palazzo* type (with its superimposed orders) derive from Venetian constructions whose façades are characterised by a pronaos.

The 17th and 18th century villa repeats already consolidated types. Maximum value is accorded the central hall, which can be identified from the outside because of the raised tympanum or cupola forms. This villa is also twice the height, and is interrupted by an overhanging gallery which is flanked by doorways and windows in the upper order. Gardens and parks became important, with their wealth of little towers, exedras, citrus orchards, belvederes, mazes, grottoes and pagodas.

The monumental villa, which also coincides with the end of the Republic, is characteristic of the 18th century and the evolution of the villa-*palazzo*. At the end of the villa period we have Palladian-like neo-classicism, and in particular the architecture and gardens of Giuseppe Jappelli, and we might consider as the final examples of the Veneto villa (even though admittedly quite distant from the initial model) those that were built in the final quarter of the 19th century. These were often residences for the new middle class, and no longer for the mainland nobility or Venetian patricians.

Province of Belluno

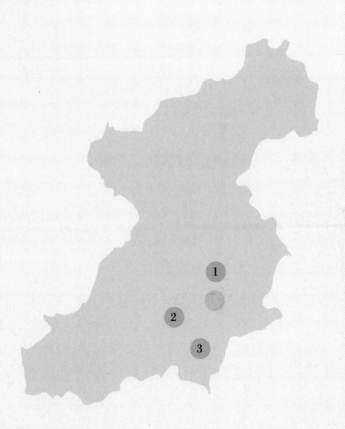

1 – Villa Fulcis, Montalban

Cusighe, Safforze

The villa, which is an imposing building set against the summit of Mount Serra, was build in the 16th or 17th centuries by the Fulcis family, who then sold the villa to the Montalban counts in the mid 19th century.

The main body has three floors (ground, *piano nobile* and mezzanine); the ground floor has two lateral lines of small rectangular windows, while

the central floor opens with a portico with coupled Tuscan columns with five arches. The *piano nobile* has a series of centred windows, and a three-light balcony over the central arch of the lower portico. The mezzanine has almost squared windows and a three-light mullioned window aligned with the lower window, and, just above, a three-light mullioned dormer window and pilasters, crowned with a tympanum and linked with volutes. The side wings, developed on two levels, are extremely simple.

2 – Villa Rudio, Milanesi
Sedico, Landris

The villa deploys several elements taken from Venetian architecture. It has two floors and a mezzanine, two lines of centred windows along each side, with a plain overhanging cornice and a central main doorway displaying the same type of finish, flanked by two square holes. The windows repeat the same form, albeit on a larger scale, along the *piano nobile*, at the centre of which there is a three-light window with balcony. There are square openings along the mezzanine, with a central three-light window with similar holes, even though they are higher. Centred three-light dormer window, a tympanum with a central *oculus* and acroterial vases, Venetian reverse-bell chimneys. A gradually sloping ramp leads to the entrance via the garden. The interior contains pictorial and stucco decorations.

Province of Padua

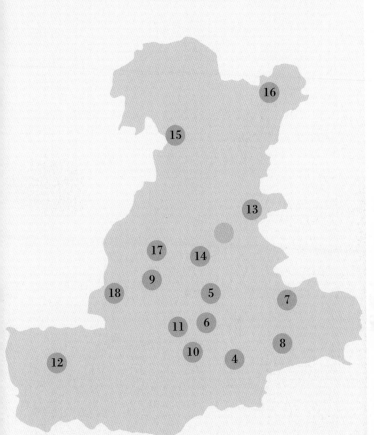

4 – Villa Widmann

Bagnoli di Sopra, Borletti, piazza Marconi 43

In 1656 the Widmann family bought the buildings and land belonging to a monastery after its dissolution. In the 1670s they had a villa built on the site, based on a project by Baldassarre Longhena. The villa is in the town square (it was probably originally built *around* the square), and it has a long, monumental façade, with a grandiose overhanging loggia along the main section. Behind the villa there is a French-style garden, with hornbeam hedges that have been shaped into exedra chambers. Here there are 160 statues (the more important ones by Antonio Bonazza), commissioned by Lodovico Widmann in 1742. The garden has been seen as a theatrical space since the Humanistic period, but here the garden is filled with actors from the *Commedia dell'Arte*, even though there are a few mythical and allegorical figures. In fact, the villa became famous as for its theatrical representations, with Carlo Goldoni both writing and acting.

5 – Casa d'Este, also known as "Castello del Catajo"
Battaglia Terme, Catajo, via Catajo

The Catajo complex takes its name from the town it was built in, surrounded by mount Sieva, along the Brenta river, at the foot of the Euganean hills. Its roots lie in an original villa whose loggia looked onto the canal, where the extremely cultivated Beatrice Pia degli Obizzi held an exclusive literary salon. Her son Pio Enea I, a man-at-arms for the Serenissima, fell in love with the view offered from the surrounding hill, where he added a tower-*cum*-belvedere with rooms frescoed by Giovan Battista Zelotti depicting his father's and forebears' war victories. Andrea Della Valle oversaw the building from about 1570 to 1573. The exterior was fortress-like, with little towers, battlements, triumphal arches and drawbridge. The imposing construction behind the building, thus determining two levels, required an enormous amount of work in terms of levelling and terracing. A large park situated among gentle hills and valleys, and crossed by the Rialto stream, was used for hunting. The Marquis Pio Enea II also appreciated the property – so much so in fact that when he inherited it in 1648 he spent the next 18 years extending and restructuring it. In 1803 the last of the Obizzi family, Tommaso, bequeathed it to the Duke of Modena, but not before adding collections of weaponry, coins, paintings, musical instruments and archaeological finds. Under the Hapsburgs (who built extensions to the villa, even though they moved the collections to Vienna), the villa had as many as 350 rooms in the four-storey building.

The grounds have a series of 17th and late 16th century scenic fountains, including the magnificent Elephant Fountain. There are also statues, masks, large aviaries, a hedge-maze, a 17-arch loggia near the canal, hanging gardens, loggias, terraces, a fishpond, swimming baths and the Giants' Courtyard, an enormous dug-out courtyard which was once used for naumachiae, tournaments and performances. The external frescoes have been destroyed.

6 – Villa Selvatico, Emo Capodilista
Battaglia Terme Sant'Elena, via dei Colli

Even though many more villas were built in the 17th century, the increase in numbers was not borne out in the external decorations. The architecture of the 17th century villa could be defined as a free combination of forms and stock decorations, sometimes leading to surprising results even though they were rarely innovative. In the Treviso area, but even more so in the Padua area, the Baroque began early, perhaps encouraged by the cultural ferment originally felt by and then fostered by the University. Villa Selvatico is confirmation of this. It was begun at the end of the 16th century, developed during the early 17th according to extremely innovative criteria which were completely devoid of reference to classical precedent, and finished in 1647. The courageous blend of the classical (two superimposed orders of Doric and Ionic half-columns and pilasters crowned with tympana) and the medieval (towers with high battlements placed at the four corners of the building), with a hint of the oriental (the blind cupola's only function is to be seen clearly from the distance), was unthinkable even only a few decades before, and is a triumph of the scenic and the suggestive.

The building was designed to be seen from its four vantage points – the opposed prospects are identical; the building is isolated and set off from the surrounding countryside by being placed on top of the small hill above the ancient thermal baths. Benedetto Selvatico had Antonio Forzan construct the seven-ramp staircase just after 1646. The staircase originally reached the Brenta, but the banks of the river were gradually raised over the years, thus modifying the villa's and the garden's relationship with the surrounding countryside. The cruciform main hall was frescoes in 1650 by Luca da Reggio. Based on Virgil's *Aeneid*, the cycle recounts the story of the Trojan hero, the mythical founder of Patavium (Roman Padua). Padovanino's octagonal painting, *The Glory of the Selvatico Household*, can be admired on the ceiling.

Agostino Meneghini, the owner who gave new impetus to the thermal baths, decided to transform the hill into an English garden and in 1816 hired Giuseppe Jappelli, an exquisitely classical architect, who brought to bear his great sensitivity and imagination.

7 – Villa Roberti, Frigimelica, Bozzolato
Brugine, via Roma 102

The villa and *barchesse* complex was built in the centre of a large property owned by the Paduan Roberti family. It was built by Andrea Della Valle between 1544 and 1551. The very simple architectural style is enhanced by frescoes both inside and outside the building by Giambattista Zelotti and his students. Other frescoes by Paolo Veronese can be found over some of the doors. The paintings in the central hall simulate a trabeated Doric order with ribbed columns which opens out onto a landscape containing scenes inspired by Ovid's *Metamorphoses*. The vestibule is dec-

orated with grotesques and landscapes and mythological figures. The most important aspects of the villa are constituted by the overall plan and the internal layout. The main entrance is made up of a semi-octagonal ramp of steps which leads to an internal loggia and three passages, then a narrow vestibule leading into the middle of the transversal hall which, though not very long, is rather wide and divides the house itself into two identically-sized sections with very similar layouts.

The villa was handed over to the Frigimelica family, including Girolamo Frigimelica, in the 17th century. The Frigimelicas added windows on the mezzanine floor along the front of the building and introduced Serliane with a double-ramp staircase at the head of the hall.

8 – Villa Garzoni, Michiel, Carraretto

Candiana, Ponte Casale, via Liston 6

Towards the middle of the 15th century, the Venetian Garzoni family bought some land south of Padua and spent the next hundred years or so extending the property, reclaiming the swampy land and improving the harvest. Finally, Alvise Garzoni decided to build a main residence, which was probably built between 1537 and 1550.

Jacopo Tatti, also known as Sansovino (1486-1570), a sculptor and architect born in Florence but who had honed his skills in Rome, came to Venice after the Sack of Rome in 1527. He introduced a classical note to the city as well as the Renaissance style that had already firmly taken hold in Papal Rome. It was Sansovino who was responsible for "modernising" St Mark's Square in Venice, which represented the power of the Serenissima, by adding the Library, the Zecca and the Loggetta.

Villa Garzoni is the only occasion in which he dedicated himself to a villa. The prospect has elements in common with the typical Venetian *palazzo*, the function of a two-dimensional stage-setting (almost as if no consideration had been given to the sides of the building) as well as the opening up of the central section between two lateral "blocks". Behind the façade, through the arches, there is a progressive breaking down - the arches are repeated; thus bringing about a perspectival view that leads into the countryside. The central section is therefore devoid of the typically Venetian passage hall, and has been given a Roman-style internal courtyard. The façade is made up of the usual base designed to defend the building against flooding and the servants' quarters. There are two *piani nobili*; with three lines of centred windows along the lateral wings and a central double loggia with five supporting arches framed by a trabeated semi-column order (Doric below and Ionic above). It should be noted that the Doric frieze extends along the entire façade, and is brought to an end just slightly into the sides of the building. There is a loggia just after a steep staircase and beyond the arches. The loggia repeats the same arches that lead to the square courtyard, which is surrounded by two more identical perpendicular porticoes and a wall containing windows giving onto a large orchard, which also contains the same five lines which can be found

along the façade. The loggia along the façade, therefore, by being "multiplied" in both parallel and orthogonal forms, defines the entire volume of the building. Two symmetrical rooms are developed along the sides of the loggia for the length of the loggia itself. The "depth" of the loggia also determines the size of the two symmetrical staircases and the *enfilade* of three interlinked rooms on either side and which give onto the courtyard. The portico also contains a terrace with balustrade and 18th century statues. The floor of the hanging courtyard was designed with slopes and undulations so that the rain water would collect in the central well, with its cistern in the lower reaches of the villa. A series of pipes originally fed the water under the ground floor in order to cool the rooms during the particularly muggy summers. The same pipes then led the water into the garden.

Fireplaces and sculptures by Sansovino can be found in the interior.

In the final analysis, this building is dominated by a taste for *inventio* and by a passion for Roman architectural style: while from the outside the building appears massive, from the inside it nonetheless turns out to be an almost choral-like compendium of open and semi-open spaces, which relegates the few closed rooms to a rather reduced space along the side wings. It is particularly appropriate, therefore, as a summer residence.

The courtyard was converted into a fully-fledged garden in the 18th century following the lines of the architectural axes of the prospect, and was provided with statues.

The entrance to the rustic courtyard is via a Mannerist portal, where the classical forms have been fragmented and then recomposed.

9 – Villa Barbarigo, Pizzoni Ardemani

Galzignano Terme, Valsanzibio, via Diana

The complex, situated in the little hollow of Sant'Eusebio in the eastern Euganean hills, is surrounded by a series of pretty hills forming an amphitheatre. Apart from the famous, better-preserved and – documented 18th century Venetian garden, the villa also boasts the largest and best-preserved tree-maze in Europe. The Contarini family began work on the 1500 square metre garden, but the current layout was undertaken in about 1669 by the Barbarigo brothers (Antonio, a Senator and then a Venetian Procurator, and Gregorio, Bishop of Padua who was later beatified). The area is divided into squares by a longitudinal axis about 400 meters long which, passing through the villa, continues right up to the summit of the hill, which is intersected by a transversal axis at the lowest point of the

grounds and by other perpendicular axes. Arbours, belvederes, exedras, aviaries, hornbeams, cerris, ilexes, oaks, elms and cypresses sre used to create set walkways, little clearings and winding paths. The statues are both beautiful and symbolic: the island of rabbits, the swan fountain (symbols of fecundity and purity), the Hill of Time, the small red marble octagonal fountain with its numerous statues and the *piazza* with its little fountains. The square maze of thick box-tree hedges is a concentration of allegories and allusions. It covers an area of about 3000 square metres, and its concentric and parallel walks run to a whole 1.5 kilometres. The entire length has to be broached in its entirety to reach the centre (the structure reflects our earthly condition, and the various trials and tribulations which have to be overcome before reaching paradise). The interesting Bath of Diana, with its many statues, was originally the watery entrance placed at the extremity of the transversal axis.

The villa, which is very small if compared to the overall complex, follows the more traditional scheme of the 17th-18th century Veneto villa.

10 – Villa Cortuso, Maldura, Emo Capodilista
Monselice, Rivella, via Padova 4

The villa was built in 1588 and is generally attributed to Vincenzo Scamozzi. It is constituted by a very simple isolated block, a slightly raised storey which can be reached by a set of lateral staircases which form a link between the storey and a tetrastyle pronaos with a tympanum with coat-of-arms, and a series of columns with terracotta Corinthian capitals.

This was originally the main prospect of the building, and faced the Battaglia canal, with which it was linked by a small causeway. The villa was originally higher than the original banks of the canal, but, as the banks themselves were raised over the years, the villa is now much lower than the banks (the same is true for many other complexes built along canals and rivers).

The garden has recently been restructured, and two original fish-ponds have been restored.

11 – Villa Duodo, Balbi, Valier

Monselice, via Sette Chiesette

The Duodo estate can be reached through an arched portal, the Porta Romana, which stands at the end of the so-called Via Del Santuario, which winds its way up the hill and leads to the Rocca di Monselice.
Pietro Duodo, who was sent by Venice to the Holy See, was given permission in 1592 to demolish a nun's convent and use the grounds to build

the villa and the new San Giorgio church (which he built with his friend Vincenzo Scamozzi – completed in 1605). The church is also the last of the "Stations of the Cross", which are constituted by six small chapels (all built later than San Giorgio), called the seven Roman basilicas (excluding St Peter's). Thanks to a privilege granted by Pope Paul V in 1605, pilgrims who visited all seven churches were guaranteed the same indulgences as those visiting the Roman basilicas. Andrea Tirali (1657-1737), the architect responsible for the churches of San Nicola da Tolentino and

San Vidal in Venice, built a new wing in the *piazzetta* onto which Scamozza's villa and church faced. He added statues and reliefs to the original Serliane on the villa façade, which conferred an excessive theatricality in the attempt to insert excessive elements onto what was basically a plain form. Towards the Rocca there is a grandiose exedra with an imposing 18th century staircase. The exedra surrounds the *piazza*, and has a central fountain. Busts by Alessandro Vittoria of three members of the Duodo family adorn a series of niches.

12 – Villa Pisani, Placco

Montagnana, Borgo San Zeno, via Borgo Eniano 1

The villa was built in the 1650s by Andrea Palladio for Francesco Pisani. The site, just in front of Porta Padova and just beyond the city walls, imposed the rigidly cubic form and the return to the two *piani nobili* form, giving the building the aspect of a small suburban *palazzo*.

The part facing the road has been given a double tetrastyle order (Ionic

over Doric) of semicolumns which, without any overhang (the presence of the road made this impossible), highlight the central section, crowned by a tympanum with a coat-of-arms held up by two winged genies by Alessandro Vittoria.

The styleme is repeated on the opposite façade, facing the garden (even though here there are loggias with free columns), and corresponds to an internal vaulted room with four columns, with niches containing statues by Vittoria dedicated to the four seasons.

13 – Villa Giovanelli

Noventa Padovana, via Cappello 241

The villa, probably built by Antonio Gaspari in the late 17th century, has one very high storey and two mezzanine floors. There are four very simple axes per side while the three central axes are protected by a colossal hexastyle Corinthian pronaos on columns, crowned by a tympanum with coat-of-arms and acroterial statues, with a semi-octagonal base. In 1738 Giorgio Massari added a grandiose staircase, containing six statues along the balustrade. The statues are by Antonio Tarsia, Antonio Gai and Marino Groppelli. The double-height main hall contains frescoes by Giuseppe Angeli (the frescoes are currently in a very poor state), stuccoes framing paintings and large medallions in the side rooms. The garden was laid out in 1738. It was originally quite famous, but very little is still extant.

14 – Villa Molin, Capodilista, Conti, Dondi dell'Orologio, Kofler

Padua, Mandriola, via Ponte della Cagna 106

Vincenzo Scamozzi began work on the villa in 1597. It was commissioned for the ambassador Nicolò Molin, and was erected on the banks of the Battaglia canal near the Cagna bridge. The building has a central, squared plan, with a square room at its centre, whose side is at a ratio of 1:2 with the outer perimeter of the villa, which is developed upwards, emerging with a square-based body with a thermal window per side providing the lighting. The prospect facing the canal is enhanced by a starkly jutting Ionic pronaos, containing a coat-of-arms in the tympanum, whose horizontal frame follows the overhang, and with acroterial statues. This imposing form shifts the building's fulcrum and modifies its centrality, underlining its orientation towards the canal. The other sides, in fact, are very different, and contain only very simple Serliane. The ashlar socle was lost when the grounds were raised, which often happened to villas built along the canal.

The main hall is completely frescoed. The garden by Scamozzi is still extant, and contains 18th century statues and a fountain. The park and courtyard are also still extant.

During the First World War the villa was used as a military command post, and it was here that the Armistice agreement was written up. The Armistice document was later signed at Villa Giusti in 1918.

15 – Villa Contarini, Camerini

Piazzola sul Brenta, via Luigi Camerini 1

This is one of the most grandiose buildings in the area. The central block of the building was designed by Palladio in 1546 for Francesco and Piero Contarini.

In 1676 Marco Contarini, a Procurator for St Mark's, began to radically transform the building. He began with the decorations for the central section, added the side wings and *barchesse* and transformed the east wing into a gallery with atlases over a rustic order, covered by a statue-laden

terrace. There are more statues in the garden, and along the fish-pond balustrade and in the niches along the nymphaeum.

The villa was not designed simply as a "site for delights", or humanistic *otii* as opposed to *negotii*: the artificial canal that flows through the garden was used to irrigate the rice paddies, turn the mills, and provide water for the silk production. In 1680, Marco Contarini designed the large hemicyclical *piazza* in front of the villa, with its portico resting on heavy rustic columns. It was eventually completed in the mid-17th century. There were also two theatres, a concert hall with an innovative acoustic structure, frescoes, a dance hall, stuccoes by Temanza (1770), a circular Neo-

classical oratory, an art gallery, a plaster gallery, a stone museum, a map museum, a library and a modern art museum. In 1868, the garden in front of the main façade was redesigned with large lawn *parterres* and a central fountain by Eugenio Mastri for Luigi Camerini; the back garden was designed by Lupati and Oblach in 1892 for Paolo Camerini. Up to 1924 Piazzola was considered a model city, with its important industrial plants and workers' houses set amongst gardens and orchards. Visitors can still admire the original lake with its own island. The current aspect reflects the heavy Baroque style of the Contarini family and the Art Nouveau and eclectic styles deployed by the Camerini family.

16 – Villa Cornaro, or Corner
Piombino Dese, via Roma 35

Andrea Palladio put together the design in the 1650s for the Venetian patrician Giorgio Cornaro, but the villa was not completed until after the end
of the 17th century. The model recalls the only other Palladian work
dating from the same period, Villa Pisani in Montagnana, even if Villa
Cornaro actually allowed for a much freer development of the original plan.
The double order of Corinthian over Ionic loggias gradually broadens

and forms a hexastyle as it juts out beyond the side wings (which, in their turn, spread out symmetrically from the central block). The loggia is repeated within the building, towards the back, at the point of the central staircase . This loggia has four columns, with statues by Camillo Mariani (1593-1595) adorning the niches. Unlike the vaulted ceiling of the first loggia, this ceiling has been given a plain beam finish. The villa also contains four hundred frescoes by Mattia Bortoloni (1717) for Andrea Cornaro, stuccoes by Bortolo Cabianca, as well as a garden containing a wealth of flower beds, fish-ponds, porticoes and loggias.

17 – Villa Emo Capodilista

Selvazzano Dentro, Feriole, Montecchia, via Montecchia 11

This villa is truly unique because of its perfectly symmetrical central plan. The Montecchia plateau and the surrounding land had belonged to the Capodilista family for centuries, and in 1568 Gabriele asked the painter and architect Dario Varotari (1534-1596). Varotari, who was at that time working on a cycle of frescoes in the nearby Praglia abbey, originally planned it as a hunting lodge, but the building was later also used as a theatre because of its scenic qualities.

Varotari had the top of the hill flattened, creating a square-shaped Italian-style garden, with quadrilobed side axes. The same axes were then extended to the stairs at the very heart of the building to form a central cross. These stairs then form a right angle and continue along the perpendicular axis and eventually lead to the loggias on the upper floor along the other two sides of the building. The end result is a perfectly square form, with four double five-arched loggias, among Doric ashlar lesenes along the ground floor, four small angular faux towers, a central crossed staircase forming four square rooms on both floors. Along the perfectly identical prospects, the little towers are somewhat hidden and toned down by linking volutes and Oriental and fable-like decorative elements.

Varotari frescoed the rooms of the villa along with Antonio Vassillacchi (also known as Aliense – 1556-1692). The so-called "Room of the Villas" depicts other villas owned by the family, and elegant *rocaille* motifs were added in the 18th century. The gentle slope of the hill was later given a tree-lined park. Near the villa there is still a medieval castle with an imposing central tower and a small 16th century church. The courtyard now houses a restaurant and a museum on the history of rural life in the area. Tradition has it that the castle was the site of a difficult meeting between St Anthony and Ezzelino da Romano. Giordano Forzatè, later beatified and one of the Capodilista family's forebears, was also present. The noble Paduan Capodilista family eventually married into the patrician Emo family from Venice, thus giving rise to the Emo-Capodilista line.

18 – Villa Olcese, also known as "The Villa of the Bishops"
Torreglia, Luvigliano, via dei Vescovi

The villa seems to have been commissioned by the Venetian bishop Francesco Pisani, and through the humanist Alvise Cornaro (who was his administrator between 1529 and 1538) Giovanni Maria Falconetto (1468-1534), who had also successfully worked in Padua for Cornaro, was eventually asked to work on the villa. Building thus began around the 1530s and was probably completed in about 1542 by Andrea Della Valle, responsible for the *barchesse* and the surrounding wall with monumental portals, reverse-arched wall and stone spheres (similar to Villa Badoer and Villa Garzoni). The villa was built in one of the most panoramic areas of the Euganean Hills, along a ridge where a medieval castle once stood (in fact, the villa makes use of the original castle foundations). The natural slopes are used to create steps and terraces, which, along with the *barchesse*, form an interesting whole. The villa is an imposing two-storey square-planned block, which is "lightened" by various openings which give onto the surrounding landscape. The ground floor has an ashlar finish, with arches on pilasters and multi-ramp stair-cases which form complex architectural motifs along the two main, and opposite, sides. The ground floor actually seems much more like a high basement sustaining a single storey, which is clearly distinguishable from

the rest. The upper floor has been given a five-arched loggia structure on piers framed by Doric lesenes, and by paired lesenes at its extremities. The interior was completely frescoed, apparently by Lambert Sustris from Amsterdam, and has been partly restored. The rooms are not distributed symmetrically, and the villa still contains the Venetian-style passage hall, with its two extremities in the two loggias (with which it forms a double "T"), thus doubling the model for Venetian *palazzi* which had only one main prospect, and perpendicular side rooms.

Province of Rovigo

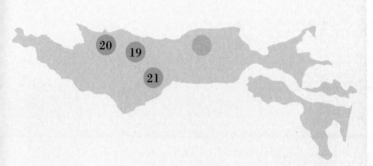

19 – Villa Badoer, also known as "La Badoera"
Fratta Polesine, via Tasso 1

The project for the villa dates from about 1556. It was undertaken by Palladio for the Venetian senator Francesco Badoer, and was completed in about 1568-1570. The villa still contains frescoes by Giallo Fiorentino. The villa is characterised by an imposing hexastyle Ionic pronaos which is reached via a large staircase which has a first level (leading onto a terrace which runs around the entire building) which originally had a wellhead and well, and two side ramps which lead to the Tuscan-style exedra porticoes. This is the first of its type, and along with the building, the porticoes separate the court with its two fountains from the back garden (no longer extant). The surrounding wall with reverse arches and stone spheres was built at the same time as Andrea Della Valle's in the Villa dei Vescovi in Luvigliano. This latter villa actually inspired the entire Villa Badoer project, and especially the fact that the kitchen and laundry areas were the base on which the rest of the villa was then constructed.

20 – Villa Molin, Bragadin, Grimani, Guerrini, Avezzù
Fratta Polesine, via Zabarella 1

This Palladio-inspired villa, based on the adjacent Villa Badoer, whose setting it in some respects completes, and even more on Villa della Malcontenta, was built between the mid- and late-16th century. Like Villa Badoer, it too was frescoed by Giallo Fiorentino.

It is made up of a main volume preceded by a hexastyle Doric pronaos,

where the crowning tympanum nonetheless goes no higher than the attic storey (that is, no higher than the overhang), thus limiting the sense of extreme verticality of the building. The same effect is given by the double windows of the side wings, even though it must be said that the windows are too close to the pronaos on the one hand and the corner of the building on the other, quite the opposite of the Palladian model, which had only once central series of windows. The pronaos, which is placed on a socle, is underscored by five ashlar arches, with side steps.

21 – Villa Morosini, Mantovani
Polesella, via Alessandro Selmi

Tradition has it that this, the southern-most of the Veneto villas on the Po River, was built for the Santo Stefano line of the Morosini family by Vincenzo Scamozzi at the end of the 16th century. It was much higher than the banks of the river, to which it was directly linked. The constant flooding forced local authorities to raise the level of the flood banks, eventu-

ally leaving the villa "stranded" much lower than the banks themselves. The villa extends in breadth along a *piano nobile* and two mezzanine floors; it has three axes per side and a central section with a tetrastyle Ionic pronaos with semi-columns and three arches crowned by a tympanum and a later Baroque fastigium. A wide staircase links the pronaos the the surrounding grounds. The large central hall, along with the other rooms, still contains late 16th century and Baroque decorations, heavy stuccoes, enormous fireplaces with allegorical figures and 17th century drapery.

Province of Treviso

22 – Villa Tiepolo, Passi

Carbonera, Vascon, Castello, via Brigata Marche 26

This complex, built by the Senator and Procurator of St Mark's Almorò Tiepolo, is constituted by a villa with symmetrical lateral adjacent buildings which then form a right angle and are linked with the main body of the building by double loggias along three axes. The whole forms a large courtyard with flowerbeds and a central fountain, and is set in a park containing a small temple, stables, two hot-houses, fountains, a small lake, busts, ornamental vases and statues attributed to Giuseppe Bernardi (also called "Il Torretti" – 1694-1774), Antonio Canova's teacher.

The villa itself is an early 17th century "block" which is perfectly in keeping with the style of Venetian *palazzi*: there are central three-light windows with balcony and two two-light windows on either side with a small balustrade; the central doors (both lower and upper) are arched, with adjacent architraved windows and upper windows, forming a typically and decidedly Venetian styleme that recalls the superimposition of two Serliane. The ground floor has rectangular windows, while the *piano nobile* has cambered windows; up to this point all levels correspond perfectly to those of the adjacent buildings, which, however, only have architraved windows. But the villa also has a third floor, which it is believed was added later, or at least partly raised, towards the end of the 18th century, with the rectangular windows of the ground floor and the small balustrades on the second floor, and, to top it off, an attic with a cambered single-light window, lesenes, a small crowning fronton and linking Baroque volutes. The loggias linking the building with the side wings are also thought to date from the late 18th century. The three-light window of the *piano nobile* corresponds to the central hall, as is always the case in Venetian *palazzi*; the hall is decorated with 18th century frescoes depicting mythological subjects in perspective paintings and stuccoes dating from the 18th century. The furnishings and décor are also 17th and 18th century. The small church is adorned with Venetian stuccoes and a marble altar with an altar-piece depicting Saints Domenico and Gaetano. The ceiling fresco is *La fede* (*The Faith*). To the side of the church there is a bell-tower with a small cupola and clock.

23 – Villa Zeno, also called "Il Donegal"

Cessalto, Donegal, via Donegal 11

The villa was built for the patrician Marco Zeno before 1566, and is based on designs by Andrea Palladio. It can be found in his *Quattro libri dell'architettura*, albeit in a noticeably different form. This is a two-storey block which has been extended in breadth, with small rectangular windows and string-course strips. The prospect giving onto the garden is "opened up" in the central area by three high arches on pilasters, which are crowned

by a simple tympanum above the corresponding cornice, which is reflected on the opposite prospect. This latter prospect has axes which do not correspond to the former. There are four axes, plus the door between two windows, in the section beneath the fronton, and a further two on each side. Both the outside and the interior of the villa are dominated by the concept of harmonious Palladian proportion, despite the extreme overall simplicity. If compared to the design, what are missing above all are a thermal window on the main prospect and the *barchesse*, which are linked to the villa via a "U"-shaped portico on trabeated columns, forming a courtyard.

24 – Villa Tamagnino, Negri, Lattes
Istrana, Casoni, via Nazario Sauro 50

The villa, which was constructed in 1715 for Count Paolo Tamagnino, was one of Giorgio Massari's first works. Massari himself later lived in the villa, which was then inherited by the Counts Negri, who passed it onto the Lattes family in the mid-19th century. Massari, a Venetian, is considered a transitional figure between the Palladian tradition, which he reconsidered in the light of Baldassarre Longhena's work, and Neo-Classicism. This building, however, appears to be rather Baroque because of the extreme verticality of the central section, which prevails over the composed feel of the elements deployed along the lower levels. The two-storey main residence in fact extends to include a third floor, with a Serliana breaking into the crowning tympanum, only in the middle section, linked with the second floor by two arched wings which extend to the corners of the building, rounded off by stone spheres on plinths. All of the middle sections seems to be integrally extrapolated from the façade of a typically Venetian *palazzo*,

with the Serliane surmounted by a square cornice. To the sides of the building, two symmetrical arched *barchesse* on exedra-style pilasters embrace, along with the small surrounding wall, the oval Italian garden, which contains statues, ponds and a chapel to the south-east, with an altar-piece and ceiling by Amigoni, a high-relief containing a portrait of Tamagnino and two paintings from the Piazzetta school. The *barchesse*, linked to the central body by an arcade on each side, crowned by a terrace delimited by a balustrade with *putti* on each corner, contain two wrought iron Dogal coats-of-arms of the Dolfin family, a fountain with two columns and

putti surmounted by a marble coat-of-arms with a seal conceded by Napoleon to a member of the Lattes family. At the back of the villa there is a fruit orchard with fish-ponds and statues, amongst which the busts of the twelve Caesars. The villa, which is richly furnished, contains art collections of mainly Eastern art, with many rare pieces, an art gallery, a collection of clocks, an extravagant collection of carillons and mechanical toys, musical instruments, a portrait (probably the only one) of Giorgio Massari, an interesting kitchen with authentic furniture and bric-a-bracs – almost all of which was collected by the last owner, Bruno Lattes.

25 – Villa Barbaro, Basadonna, Manin, Giacomelli, Volpi
Maser, Strada Comunale Bassanese

The territory of Maser (which was fought over by Belluno, Treviso and Feltre in the medieval period) was taken over by the Barbaro family in 1339. Palladio was asked to build the villa in about 1560 by the brothers Daniele (an Ambassador of the Republic to England and then patriarch of Aquileia; Daniele then translated and provided the commentary and notes for Vitruvius' *De architectura*, a fundamental architectural text for the Renaissance, and in fact the only surviving ancient text on the subject, which was illustrate by Palladio himself) and Marcantonio (ambassador, senator, Governor of the Mainland, Procurator of Sopra, Superintendent to the Arsenale, Salt Superintendent and amateur sculptor), mainly for the latter's holidays with his consort Giustiniana Giustinian and their four children. The complex, set on the slopes of the Asolo hills, is very different from Palladian villa productions: it is not built on a plain in the middle of a family's plot of land, but to the margins and on a slight slope; it does not respect the hierarchical scheme for buildings according to their functions, so that the owner's rooms in part continue on into the *barchesse*, which were usually used for exquisitely rustic reasons; and the side pigeon-coops, masked by the façades with sun-dials crowned by a tympanum and reverse-arched side links, vie with the jutting central body of the main residence, which has no free-column pronaos but is framed by a tetrastyle Ionic order of semi-columns and an exaggeratedly large tympanum, with trabeation interrupted by the central balcony, with its stucco high-relief showing the family coat-of-arms. The horizontal plan of the building is reminiscent of Villa Emo in Fanzolo. It seems that this can all be attributed to the commissioners' own wishes. They wanted to recreate a classical villa, based on the descriptions Pliny offered of his own Villa Laurentina and on modern interpretations of the ancient in 16th century Rome. The Eternal City is clearly being evoked with the nymphaeum: behind the building there is a small, rectangular secret garden, with a semi-elliptical pool at its centre which leads to a circular grotto, containing the statue of a river deity distributing the waters from the source just behind the statue. This same source provides the water for the fountains and fish-ponds, and irrigates

the orchards. In fact, water is one of the characterising elements of the entire complex. The whole building is amply decorated with stuccoes and sculptures by Alessandro Vittoria (except for some of the minor decorative elements, which may well have been by Marcantonio) and paintings by Veronese. The river deity, which became one of the *topoi* of the Roman garden after the first example in the Vatican's Belvedere courtyard, is completely new for the Veneto. The other typically Roman element is the small temple which can be found along the road to the south-east. Dated to 1580, and based on a circular plan, it is a mini-Pantheon demonstrating the same cubic proportions and similar elements, the same pronaos, the graded cupola, apses alternating with aediculae within, with stucco statues by Vittoria and two external statues outside the temple in soft stone by Orazio Marinali. There are also signs of the chapel in the Castle of Anet, by Philibert de L'Orme. The exceptional nature of the complex is further heightened by the pictorial cycle on the *piano nobile*. The cycle was painted by Paolo Veronese, assisted by his brother Benedetto and other students from their workshop. The iconographic programme seems to have been dictated by the commissioners, and Daniele in particular, who was one of the most refined humanists of the period: the dominant motif seems to be Harmony, and particularly familial harmony, the integration of mythology and Christian doctrine within a single concept of Nature; guided by the Empyrean planets, dominated by thoughts of Immortality, the life of the powerful family happily unfolds within the festive country framework. The walls are framed by an order of painted, ribbed Corinthian columns on faux marble basements and placed against the landscape, which is filled with gods from Olympus, characters taken from daily life, nudes, *putti*, statues and cameos. These can all be found in the rooms variously referred to as "of Olympus", "of the Dog", "of the oil-lamp", "the cross", the room of Bacchus and the Tribunal of Love. The Maser frescoes were to become a model for many artists, including Tiepolo and his followers, and imitated by Zelotti in Villa Emo in Fanzolo and elsewhere.

26 – Villa Giustinian, Salice
Portobuffolè, via Giustinian 11

This is a monumental complex from the second half of the 17th century.
Apart from the villa, it also contains *barchesse*, farm housing, the church
of St Theresa, statues, the wall that originally delimited a large park which
has since been given over to farming, entrances with statues, and the entrance
with steps on the Livenza, the course of which has since been modified.
The large villa is characterised by two double axes and a single external
axis per side, with a restricted central section with a marked verticality. The
first and last floor have the same rectangular windows, while the *piano*

nobile has a series of cambered windows and a horizontal cornice above. In the central section, on the ground floor, there is the entrance and Venetian-style rectangular windows which are directly linked to the upper balcony with three-light windows and a single plain cornice above, a neutral strip and, above, breaking into the overhang, a Serliana with balustrade which gives light to an attic, crowned with a tympanum with acroterial vases. Inside the villa there is an imposing hall decorated with stuccoes, elaborate staircases again decorated with high-relief stuccoes, and frescoed ceilings. The church, dating from 1694, has beautiful stuccoes, marbles, an 18th century fresco, a ceiling painted by Domenico Fabris (1807-1901) and a wooden crucifix attributed to Andrea Brustolon.

27 – Villa Giustinian, Ciani Bassetti
Roncade, via Roma 131-133

The villa was commissioned by the procurator Girolamo Giustinian, in
about 1489, after his marriage to Agnesina Badoer, whose family had owned
buildings and lands in the area since the 15th century. It is, however, likely
that work on the villa was not completed until about 1520 because of
the war raging against the Cambrai League on the mainland. It is thought
that the sculptor-architect Tullio Lombardo was responsible for the new
complex. The pre-existing medieval buildings have been re-evoked through
the use of the towers placed in the corners of the massive surrounding walls
with mote and small cylindrical towers at the entrance, giving the whole
a rather unusual aspect. The body of the villa belongs to the Venetian typology, with a basement, two storeys with cambered windows with simple,
plain cornice, and a mezzanine with square windows. The façade has
nine axes and is divided into three sections, of which the central section
is particularly noteworthy due to its jutting double loggia with three arcades

on columns, fan vaulted ceiling below and boxed ceiling above, crowned by a tympanum. The western and southern sides originally had external frescoes which were damaged during raids during World War II, and which were restored in 1947 by Mario Botter. In the St Anna oratory, dating from 1542-1543 and attributed to Santo Lombardo, Tullio Lombardo's son, the terracotta busts of the founders Girolamo Giustinian and Agnesina Badoer look as if they could be attributed to Jacopo Sansovino. The large courtyard in front of the villa has currently been subdivided into two English-style lawns on either side of the path that leads from the entrance bridge to the villa loggias. and is flanked by 18th century statues, and two small Italian-style gardens alongside the steps leading up to the loggia. This courtyard is delimited by the wall containing the entrance to the villa, and by two large, symmetrical side *barchesse* aligned with the wall, with an arched portico, from whose corners there extended two frescoed walls which closed off the secret side gardens right up to the small, square orchard. All of this was then surrounded by the larger orchard.

28 – Villa Di Rovero

San Zenone degli Ezzelini, via Bordignon 3

The central body of the villa respects the classical canons of the Veneto country home (two *piani nobili*, a mezzanine with a central three-light window), and is dated to the end of the 16th century or the early 17th. There are two symmetrical loggias, with seven arches on small columns, to the side of the villa along the second level. These lead to two square tow-

ers which are raised in the mezzanine. These form an overall harmonious whole dominating the valley. The setting is particularly picturesque – the villa is on a small hill with a view over other hills sloping towards little green valleys. On the upper floor, behind the villa, there are the remains of the Ezzelini castle, which was destroyed in 1260. There is a narrow set of steps which crosses a citron-tree garden.

There is also a beautiful park with a small church, *barchesse* and pigeon-coop. Frescoes from the Veronese school adorn the main hall.

28 – Villa Emo

Vedelago, Fanzolo, via Stazione 5

The very old Emo family, already present in Venice in 997, originally came from Greece. During a meeting of Venice's Maggior Consiglio in 1297, the family was enlisted into the patrician class, and throughout the ages the family provided the Republic with eminent figures occupying positions of responsibility in local government. The family has always owned the villa, and has always lived there.

In 1535, Leonardo Emo, Superintendent for the Mainland, lieutenant in the Veneto armed forces and Governor of Friuli in the city of Udine, bought a plot of land of about 40 hectares from Andrea Barbarigo. He irrigated the land by using the water from the nearby canal, which channelled water from the nearby Brentella river. He thus converted the sorghum production to corn. Leonardo then decided to have an appropriate building con-

structed on the site, both as a holiday retreat and for agricultural purposes, for his own family, for the peasants, the livestock and harvest; the building is therefore not simply for noble *otii*. However, it was not Leonardo who actually realised the rather innovative ideas (he was already dead by 1539), but rather his grandson Leonardo, the male heir to his dead son Alvise who, in 1556, at the age of about 20, had the Palladian villa erected. Villa Emo and Villa Barbaro in Maser are the only Palladian villas with a rectilinear disposition for both the residential and farming areas. The central body has no jutting pronaos but an internal tetrastyle Tuscan loggia; the family coat-of-arms, by Alessandro Vittoria, can be seen in the tympanum, which in this case crowns only the loggia. The villa has only one *piano nobile*, raised on a very high socle, which leads to the atrium via a long ramp. The base cornice continues along the strip of the *barchesse* arches which are placed symmetrically to the main block, with eleven arches per side, and lead to two pigeon-coops (these, however, are not as elegant as those of the Maser villa, but are two simple towers on a square base which jut out above the roof of the farm buildings below).

The *piano nobile* was completely frescoed by Giambattista Zelotti, one of Veronese's students, probably between 1561 and 1565. The frescoes are framed by architectural motifs, mainly ribbed Corinthian columns, and progress from the atrium dedicated to Ceres, or perhaps Pale, to the vestibule, the main hall, the room dedicated to Venus and another to Hercules, two small rooms of grotesques, the room dedicated to Jove and Io, traditionally reserved for the mistress of the household, and finally to the latter room's symmetrical counterpart, the room dedicated to the Arts, or the Lyceum or Muses, which was reserved for the master. In this room Architecture points in an open book to a plan of the building, and indicates the exact site of the room in question.

The furnishings are original 17th and 18th century. Currently, the villa houses a collection of peasant implements, a restaurant with rooms and swimming pool set in a large park, and an Italian garden with walkways, flowerbeds and statues.

Province of Udine

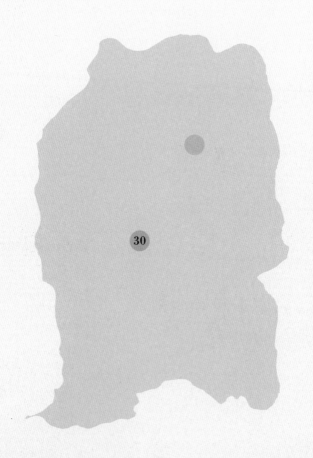

30 – Villa Manin

Codroipo, Passariano

In the second half of the 18th century, the last and greatest of the Veneto villas were built, representing Venice's farewell to the mainland. 19th century production was to be limited mainly to the building of country houses for the mainland's bourgeoisie, with more an apparent than formal link with the otherwise entrenched tradition of the villa. Villa Manin is, in a

sense, doubly symbolic of the fall of the Republic. Its owner, the last Doge Lodovico Manin, announced the end of the Serenissima Republic on May 12th, 1797, and in his villa, which had become his headquarters, Napoleon signed the Treaty of Campo Formio on October 17th. The majestic complex was begun at the end of the 17th century and completed in about the mid-18th century, perhaps by Domenico Rossi, who at the same time was working for the same commissioners on the Gesuiti church in Venice and the Duomo in Udine. The entrance, to the south, is constituted

by a bridge over a large fish-pond, flanked by two towers which also mark the beginning of two wings of porticoed *barchesse*, which form an exedra surrounding a vast lawn. Two further constructions at the ends of a transversal axis constitute a spatial pause, then another enclosure forms the main courtyard, with another two wings of rectilinear *barchesse* facing each other. This very theatrical whole then leads to the imposing body of the villa, behind and to the north of which there is another park, delimited once more by two towers, containing hothouses, fish-ponds, orange orchards, a garden, small lakes, hillocks and sculptures by Giuseppe Toretti and his assistants, Francesco Bonazza and Pietro Baratta.

The villa also contains stuccoes, tempera drawings and frescoes by Louis Dorigny and others.

Province of Venice

31 – Villa Ferretti, Angeli, Nani Mocenigo
Dolo, Sambruson, via Brenta bassa 41

Vincenzo Scamozzi signed and dated the project for the villa on August 12th, 1596, for Girolamo Ferretti, a Vicentine living in Venice. The villa was completed by 1600. The villa is built along a horizontal axis, with parallel adjacent buildings on one side and perpendicular ones on the other, and an isolated chapel. The villa complex faces the Brenta, and origi-

nally had an Italian garden with six large flowerbeds and a courtyard behind the villa. The façades are punctuated by a series of enormous Ionic lesenes and four axes per side. The three central axes, crowned by a tympanum with a central coat-of-arms, are built onto the mezzanine level, further increasing the proportions of the lesenes, and break into the overhang. The large central hall corresponds to the raised section, and there are three rooms on either side on each floor. The villa still contains remains of the original frescoes and stuccoes.

32 – Villa Rocca, Ciceri, Bressan (Hotel Villa Ducale)

Dolo, Casello Dodici, riviere Martiri della Libertà 75

The villa was built on the left bank of the Brenta, on the site where, in the 18th century, there were two "Casini Andreucci" (which were demol-

ished this century). The late 19th century construction, with its wealth of decorative elements, is preceded by an arched portico below a terrace. The statues and the oratory facing the road, however, belong to the 18th century.

33 – Villa Soranzo, also known as "La Soranza"

Fiesso d'Artico, Barbariga, via Navigli 5

Despite its name, this villa, which is situated on the left bank of the Brenta, actually belonged to the Soranzo family only between 1611 and 1671. Non-documented sources have attributed the frescoes on the façade to Benedetto Caliari (1538-1598), Paolo Caliari's brother, even though the style seems much later, overwrought as it is with masterful illusory effects and moving figures. The stuccoes and fireplaces in the villa have been attributed to Alessandro Vittoria (1518-1599). Both the internal structure and the distribution of the rooms, along with the external frescoes are perfectly in keeping with the model of the Venetian *palazzo*. There is a main "T"-shaped hall with rooms on either side, along with the typical openings along the façade which have been brought together in the Serliana centre and tightly collected between the ground and first floors. The steps and the attic with double Baroque volutes were added later.

34 – Villa Torre-Donati, Recanati, Olivieri, Zucconi, Fracasso

Fiesso d'Artico, Barbariga, via Naviglio 25

Built on the left bank of the Brenta, the villa, along with the adjacent buildings, seems to have been constructed in the early 17th century and restruc-

tured at the end of the century. The central section (slightly jutting and characterised by the central Venetian-style three-light windows) is crowned by a large fastigium with pinnacles, small frontons and interrupted, variously-curved cornices. The elliptical holes alongside the entrance arch are also typically Baroque elements.

The oratory is said to date from 1757.

35 – Villa Foscari, also known as "La Malcontenta"
Mira, Malcontenta, Moranzini, via dei Turisti 11

This is the most typical example of a villa-temple, the only Palladian one along the Brenta and in the entire province of Venice. Built for Nicolò and Alvise Foscari around 1560, after the vagaries that brought it to a state of almost total degradation, it eventually returned to the Foscari family. The villa stands alone in the middle of a large park. The main prospect of its cubic form faces north, and it is only a stone's throw away from the right bank of the Brenta. It is built on a very high socle (a Palladian expedient designed to avoid flooding – we should not forget that most of these villas are in fact built in swampy areas – and used for the general kitchen and laundry areas of the villa) and is dominated by a hexastyle Ionic pronaos with a further two lateral axes. The central axis provides two

symmetrical, right-angle sets of steps that lead to the villa proper. The apex of the fronton touches the building's overhang and is surmounted by a three-windowed attic with little lesenes and a second tympanum. This latter element is highly anomalous in Palladio's work, but it was destined to spread throughout the Treviso area. The southern façade, facing the garden, has a central section, corresponding to the pronaos, which is only barely in relief. Its tympanum is interrupted by a large thermal window, which, along with the doors beneath, suggests a large, single arch. The lateral windows and the attic are repeated. The sides are marked by three axes of simple windows, while the whole building is circumscribed by the two cornices that delimit the *piano nobile*, which is completely covered by a subdued ashlar motif.

The interior is dominated by a main cruciform hall which goes from the internal façade of the pronaos to the façade at the back of the building. The hall is flanked by six symmetrical rooms, each of which is slightly smaller than the preceding one. The *piano nobile* was entirely frescoed by Giambattista Zelotti and Battista Franco, deploying the usual system of framing within painted architectural items and ribbed Ionic columns. Over the centuries the frescoes have been ruined, and even recent work on the frescoes has been unable to restore the original aspect.

During the 17th-18th centuries the villa was extended, creating a sort of *piazza* closed off on three sides by a portico. The demolition undertaken by occupying Austrian forces in 1848 actually restored the villa's original form.

36 – Villa Seriman, Foscari Widmann – Rezzonico

Mira, Riscossa, via Nazionale 418-419-420

The villa complex can be found on the left bank of the Brenta, just in front of the *barchesse* of Villa Valmarana.

The Seriman family were Catholic Armenian merchants who arrived in Europe from Persia in the second half of the 17th century. When in 1705 Diodato Seriman married Elisabetta Tornimbeni, obtaining the lands of Mira as part of her dowry, there was already a small *palazzo* on the site. He himself built the *barchesse*, the oratory in about 1720, the garden and orchard, the surrounding wall with large statues, as well as the stables and coach-house and depot (Seriman thought of the building above all as a farming estate).

In a woodcut from about 1550-1557, Gian Francesco Costa depicts a small *palazzo* which is quite different from the current villa, even though the *barchesse* and small temple are identical.

In 1751 the Milanese Serbelloni family became the villa's new proprietors. In 1759 the villa was a low construction, but by 1782 it had assumed its current proportions. Between 1751 and 1759, the Serbelloni family had thus added the *piano nobile* and a cruciform attic with curvilinear tympana, Lombardesque windows (which were quite unusual for Venice) and had maintained the atrium and its two columns and two pilasters (even though the tympanum was eliminated).

Inside, there is an extremely high ballroom with wrought iron and brass balustrade, white and gold stuccoes depicting animals and monsters, shells and highly elaborate volutes. Some of the frescoes are thought to have been undertaken by Giuseppe Angeli (1709-1798), one of Giambattista Piazzetta's followers, and other assistants.

37 – The Villa Valmarana Barchesse

Mira, Valmarana, via Valmarana 4-15

The large 18th century property belonging to the Valmarana family, on the right bank of the Brenta, had its fulcrum in a cubic three-storey building which was devoid of any decorative motif. Two symmetrical *barchesse* derived from and were perfectly aligned with this structure, and their central body has a series of Ionic lesenes ending in a plain trabeation, and side porticoes with pilasters and coupled Tuscan columns. In the second half of the 19th century the villa was destroyed in order to evade taxes on luxury buildings; the *barchesse*, or *"foresterie"*, were then abandoned. The right *barchessa*, facing a bend in the river and thus with two of its prospects facing the Brenta, included the large hall which was frescoed in the 18th century with architectural perspectival scenes, allegories and landscapes. The frescoes have since been attributed to Michelangelo Schiavone, the "Chiozzotto" (1712-1772), from Chioggia.

38 – Villa Farsetti, Selvatico
Santa Maria di Sala, via Roma 5

18th century Venetian villas clearly reflect the mood of the Republic – they are grandiose, sometimes brash, and always offer a wealth of decorative elements.

For the first time since the advent of the Renaissance in the Veneto, decorative elements were borrowed from other European centres. Villa Farsetti, by no means an exception to this rule, recalls a French Rococo castle, with the typical physiognomy of the late "international" Baroque. It is a

three-storey building, with Doric pilaster strips, a balustrade which is symmetrically developed in alignment with the central double-height hall and whose convex line breaks into the façade area. The hall has also been given Corinthian columns and pilaster strips, and a stage for the orchestra. The two concave two-storey wings are linked by monumental 38-column porticoes in Greek marble. The columns were probably brought in from the Temple to the Goddess Concordia in Rome (in their turn taken from Greece – four of these columns can be found in the main hall), and probably given to the family by Pope Clement XIII, a distant relative of the Farsettis. Two internal flights of stairs on pilasters lead off the por-

ticoes. A rustic order *barchessa* and outer building are intentionally hidden from sight behind the villa.

The garden was a grandiose affair, with flowerbeds brimming with blooms, a citrus bower, a great number of statues, a lake with a small island, theatres, amphitheatres, bridges, streams, fish-ponds, rare vines imported along with their original loam, highly-regarded cultivation, small woods, a naumachia, a small tower, aviaries, Roman thermal baths and much more besides.

Filippo Farsetti (1703-1774), whose family, despite having been integrated into Venice, was originally from Tuscany, embraced the ecclesiastical career as a means of avoiding the political career that his rank would otherwise have demanded of him. He therefore dedicated his time to the study of arts and sciences, as well as collecting. He was a great traveller and collected many plaster reproductions of ancient statues which Antonio Canova himself studied for his own work. In 1733 Antonio inherited the Sala property, which he extended and had carefully irrigated. When he received the columns from Pope Clement XIII, he asked the Siena-born architect Paolo Posi to work them into his villa. Work was undertaken between 1758 and 1762, at the same time as the botanical gardens, which contained hothouses for citrus plants as well as many extremely rare exotic plants (amongst which the then rare *magnolia grandiflora*, which is currently so fashionable in northern Italy).

Part of the building has now been occupied by the Santa Maria di Sala local administration and the local town library.

39 – Villa Pisani, also known as "La Barbariga"

Stra, Barbariga, via Barbariga 45

In 1620 and again in 1661, the patrician Pisani dal Branco family from Venice declared themselves the proprietors of a holiday house with annexed buildings and surrounding land in the area known as "Barbariga". The building is on the right bank of the Brenta, just in front of Villa Soranza. The very first image we have of the villa comes from a print (1709 circa) by Vincenzo Coronelli, which represents what is now the central part of the villa. There is also a rustic annex, an orchard and an elementary Italian garden towards the Brenta.

Another print by Gian Francesco Costa, from about 1750, shows a villa with terraces along the side wings, the farm-house transformed into living quarters and the garden modernised. After further work on the villa, there is another representation, this time a painting by Jacopo Guarana. The central block has been decorated with light polychrome stuccoes, fireplaces with painted ceramic tiles, frescoes, windows, and delicate Oriental elements and grotesques recalling French Rococo tastes. The last additions were the two long side wings, which also contained the large ballrooms (a staple of the period). The prospect giving onto the Brenta has a simple middle fronton per side, while there is a much more imaginative prospect giving onto the garden (with its playful disposition of lesenes and coupled Ionic columns, small triangular frontons intersecting rectangular openings, alternating with elliptical oculae, and balconies, as well as the repetition of the two tympana found on the opposite prospect with acroterial vases). Apparently from the same period we also have numerous statues representing hunters and peasants, originally on the building itself and in the garden and now under the porticoes. Documents also attest to further work undertaken on the villa when the head of the household was Giannantonio Selva, who was very likely responsible for the chapel and also, perhaps, the refurbished gardens and the English-style park, with a small lake. There is also an interesting clock tower aligned with the villa on the other side of the road behind the building, presumably by Giuseppe Jappelli.

40 – Villa Cappello, Giantin

Stra, Fossolovara, via Doge Alvise Pisani 6

The building can be found between Villa Foscarini and Villa Pisani on the left bank of the Brenta. The simple 16th century construction was restructured in the 17th. The entire façade is covered in plastered ashlar. The basement has horizontal, elliptical windows, while the raised storey has cambered windows and the mezzanine rectangular ones. The central section is by far the most characteristic element: it originally had two cambered three-light windows with balconies, and the *piano nobile* was later linked directly with the grounds via a double set of stairs. The upper three-light window breaks into the overhang, and is crowned by a tympanum with acroterial pinnacles and small elements linked to another couple of flanking pinnacles.

The adjacent buildings in the park have been almost completely destroyed, and the garden has been modelled using low box-tree hedges.

41 – Villa Foscarini, Negrelli, Rossi

Stra, Fossolovara, via Doge Pisani 1

The villa was built by the Foscarini family, a patrician Venetian family, some time between 1617 and 1635. The site chosen was along the Brenta riviera just in front of the bridge that leads to San Pietro di Stra, and is flanked to the west by one of the Brenta's affluents. The building is developed laterally, and the façade is divided into three sections: the two side sections have a double central axis and a simple axis per side, while there are two obelisks on each of the two extremities of the roof aligned with the full walls. The middle section is preceded by a jutting pronaos, with a very high socle and faux ashlar covering the entire ground floor section of the façade, and an upper tetrastyle Ionic pronaos crowned by a tympanum with a plain cornice aligned with the moulding and the acroterial statues. Originally there were two sets of stairs leading from the pronaos to a raised floor along the mezzanine; the ashlar floor now forms two symmetrical wings with a large arch crowned by a balustrade terrace. These

wings, the transformation of the mezzanine into a single ground floor, new cycles of frescoes and other restoration work and readjustments are all due to the noble Negrelli family from Verona, who bought the villa in the 19th century. The prospect facing the garden reflects the prospect giving onto the Brenta, minus the ashlar and without the central jutting area. Its Ionic semi-columns are repeated along the ground floor. The guest house in the garden, with arches framed by Tuscan lesenes, was probably originally a *barchessa*, and contained two apartments and an imposing hall used for parties and receptions (there was no such hall in the main villa). It was richly frescoed by Domenico Bruni (Brescia, 1591-1666), an expert in perspectival frescoes. The figurative cycle has been attributed to Pietro Liberi. The garden also houses the stables, which were probably built by Marco Foscarini, who was the Doge of Venice from 1762 to 1763, and which are thought to have been designed by Giorgio Massari (1687-1766). They have ashlar corners, two lateral cambered ashlar doorways crowned by a small triangular fronton, two axes per side of ashlar windows, and elliptical windows along the mezzanine with subtle rectangular cornice, a central section set between vertical ashlar strips, almost stylised lesenes with a further two windows and central doorway (all ashlar), but here with a round-arch fronton. There is also a triangular tympanum with a star design and acroterial statues. The whole structure is surrounded by simple string-course strips. There is very little left of the original Italian-style garden.

42 – Villa Pisani, also known as "La Nazionale"
Stra, Fossolovara, via Doge Pisani 6

In a small bend in the Brenta, on the left bank, the Pisani di Santo Stefano family bought some property in the early 17th century. They would later build a small villa in the same area. In 1719 Girolamo Frigimelica Roberti (1653-1732) had probably finished the plans for a colossal villa for the brothers Alvise and Almorò Pisani, and to make room for this villa the preceding one was demolished in 1720. It seems that it was only in 1735, when Alvise was nominated Doge of Venice, that Francesco Maria Preti (1701-1774) was asked to put together a new project and building began on a new construction that would be completed in 1756.

Frigimelica planned the stables which can be found at the bottom of the garden. These are linked to the villa by a double tree-lined path, used as a "race-track", which was later replaced by the current pool. The stables were probably build between 1719 and 1721, and have an apparently Palladian scheme, with two exedra wings an a central hexastyle Ionic

pronaos which is, however, surmounted by a sort of attic with lesenes, a typically Baroque addition. There are innovative juttings and re-entries, exedras and ashlar arches with tympanum-like heads and a large number of statues and vases along the axes.

The villa, with its 114 rooms, is not only one of the most grandiose and elaborate of Veneto villas, but also one of the most atypical. The façade is extremely clean-cut: the central jutting area, with colossal Corinthian semi-columns, a tympanum and a festoon frieze, contains the extremely large ball room.

The ground floor is almost totally devoid of decorations, which begin

with the wooden Greek divinities (attributed to Andrea Brustolon) on the main staircase and the ceiling by Jacopo Guarana. A row of drawing rooms with corridor contain, amongst other things, paintings by Celesti, Nazzaro and Zuccarelli. There are also frescoes and paintings by Jacopo Amigoni, Fabio Canal, Giambattista Crosato, Francesco Simonini, S Ricci and Giuseppe Zais, as well as ceramics, *chinoiseries*, and glass, crystal and gilded glass lighting.

Another element from Frigimelica's project is the 10-hectare park, which is a marvellous example of the 18th century Veneto garden. Its geometric design is full of focal points and perspectival axes. It contains fish-ponds,

hothouses, a coffee house, a hexagonal exedra with curvilinear sides, maze with a small belvedere tower, farm houses, warehouses, houses, cas nos, stables, a coach-house, a house for the fire brigade, cedar-orchards i the form of galleries, an *orangerie*, an orchard, flowerbeds, statues, walk ways, *barchesse* and small woods. As in the main building, the garden also a blend of classical ideas and models that were then dominant i the rest of Europe – the secret gardens, courts and orchards, considere to be typically Venetian and used by Palladio and Scamozzi, were no longe deemed fashionable at the end of the 17th century.

At the sides of the villa there are two rustic order doorways, flanked b windows, which open up onto the surrounding wall which has been give a fake ashlar finish. The doorways frame two marble groups from the Bonz workshop (already present in 1724, that is before the villa itself and th garden as it now stands). The surrounding wall is interrupted at its Padu end by a doorway for the belvedere, which is flanked by two Corinthia columns around which the spiral wrought-iron staircase unwinds up to th terrace, with a central loggia with tympanum.

However, the villa's real masterpiece, commissioned in 1760, is the cei ing fresco in the ballroom undertaken by Giambattista Tiepolo in co laboration with his son Giandomenico, Gerolamo Mengozzi, also know as "Il Colonna" and Pietro Visconti, who finished the rest of the decora tions when Tiepolo left for Madrid on March 31st 1762. The ceiling fresc depicts the *Apotheosis of the Pisani Family*, with a cockatoo and tw male and two female Satyrs.

This is unequivocally one of Tiepolo's greatest masterpieces: here h articulates "a veritable *summa* of his art, which is magnificent in the vir tuosity of its overall vision, the supreme skill with which the work given a unitary feel, the conferring of life-like qualities on the heteroge neous whole of the most disparate allegorical figurations, the rigorous equ librium of the composition and the magnificent symphony of light an daring colour" (from *Giambattista Tiepolo: i dipinti*). The 18th centur characters, so realistic in their typical garb, almost appear to be enthralle by the allegorical nudes that surmount them and hold them aloft. The cei ing does not so much seem to symbolise the end of Venice as much as it almost preordained transfiguration from reality to legend.

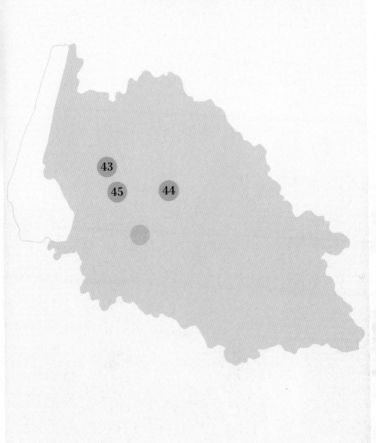

43 – Villa della Torre, Cazzola
Fumane, via Della Torre 19

In the heart of the Valpolicella district, the villa grounds form a longitudinal axis which descends from the entrance and, working its way down through the orchard and along a tree-lined walkway, continues into the entrance courtyard of the villa with.just behind, in the left-hand corner of the grounds, a small temple.The axis then continues beyond the peri-

style with its central fountain, leads to the fish-pond and its little bridge, then slopes downwards into the lower garden with an entrance to the grotto, surrounded by high walls separating the complex from two adjacent roads. This is substantially the opposite of a Palladian scheme; it is not "open" to nature, but closed in on itself, with almost insignificant external prospects while the interior is rather rich, expensive and imaginative. But the central element of the entire complex is undoubtedly the peristyle, a cultured classical reference to Roman houses. It is quite alien to the Veneto

villa model, despite its being held up by heavy pilasters made from enormous ashlars – nothing could be more rustic.

The interior was frescoed and then stuccoed, even though precious little remains except for suggestive mascarons over the fireplace.

The villa was apparently completed by 1561, and the identity of the man responsible for the original project remains a mystery. Some of the more convincing names put forward so far have been Giulio Romano and Michele Sanmicheli, both of whom were masters at using old-fashioned elements such as the rustic and grotesque elements present in this villa. However, no-one has yet to shed definitive light on the matter.

44 – Villa Allegri, Arvedi

Grezzana, Cuzzano, via Valpantena

The villa, half-way up the slope of a very picturesque hill in the Veronese pre-Alpine district, was restructured by Giovanni Battista Bianchi around 1656.In the central section there is a portico with five mixed-style arches on ashlar Tuscan columns.The portico is beneath the large balustrade terrace of the *piano nobile*, with Doric semi-columns and lesenes.The entire form breaks beyond the overhang with its fastigium with atlases, crowned by a balustrade and statues.The wings continue with symmetrical bodies on one floor with upper terraces and small towers at the summit.

Inside there are a special reception hall, a weapons room, a central hall with a ceiling that was frescoed by Louis Dorigny, a curved main staircase and 18th century furnishings.

The Italian garden facing the valley probably dates back to the second half of the 18th century.The original *parterre* is reminiscent of the French Baroque, with its very low box-tree hedges following a single design.Amongst these very large and very old box-trees (they are at least two hundred years old) there is a central fountain, a grotto with statues, more fountains with various decorative motifs and an aviary.Behind the villa there is an exedra-shaped courtyard with a scenic staircase taken from the church of San Carlo; to the sides the stables and farm-house capped off with pigeon-coop.There is also a double staircase to the north which gives onto a cypress-lined walkway which leads to the orchard.

45 – Villa Serego, Alighieri

San Pietro in Cariano, Pedemonte, Santa Sofia, via Santa Sofia 1-8

The complex was planned by Andrea Palladio for Marcantonio Serego in about 1569, but was only partly completed. It is not only the only Palladian villa in the Verona area, but above all it is the strangest of his villas. Unlike others, where his experiments usually consolidated the traditional schemes he had deployed in various villas, this villa makes use of something decidedly different. A quick look at the building offers us our first

surprise: the double portico is held up by heavy Ionic columns, with enormous archaic-style ashlar capitals.Palladio had never before used this styleme for his villas, even though, familiar as he was with the works of Michele Sanmicheli around Verona and Giulio Romano around Mantua, the use of the rustic, and above all of the rustic deftly mixed with classical elements, had had some effect on Palladio's Vicenza *palazzi*.For Villa Serego, in fact, this rustic style is "upwardly" refined and ennobled – the loggia balustrades of the loggia, with their capitals (even though the volutes are in the plain style and not diagonal, they have none the less been

expertly sculpted) lead to the triumph of the trabeation, with a three-tiered architrave, and a finely-decorated frieze.There are, however, examples of the Palladian logic at work: in the original project the porticoes had been thought of in terms of the agrarian functions of the building, and their aspect was therefore "rustic"; what's more, the different extensions of the building opened out onto the countryside, thus underlining the building's fusion with surrounding Nature.

But if, up to this point, the main reference points seem to be Palazzo Te by Giulio Romano and, even more overtly, Villa Della Torre, which has been attributed alternately to Giulio Romano himself and Sanmicheli, a comparison with the drawings in *I quattro libri di architettura* underlines even more strikingly Palladio's indebtedness to these two buildings.In fact, on the other side of the *barchesse*, Palladio had planned a rectangular peristyle with central fountain, that is an element taken directly from Ancient and Renaissance Rome and used in both of the above-mentioned buildings.In the Palladian variant, where the fourth wing is closed off by a wall (even though here there are four porticoed sides), the villa also recalls the magnificent Villa Garzoni by Jacopo Sansovino, the Florentine-Roman maestro of ancient stylemes.Beyond the peristyle there is a columned exedra with a second fountain which closes of the perspectival view.

The Palladian fragment was later placed within a garden and park with statues.

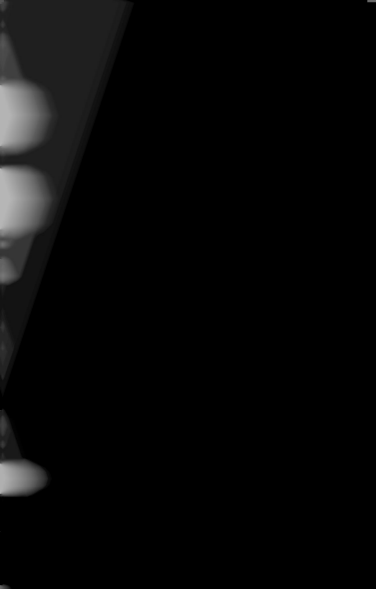

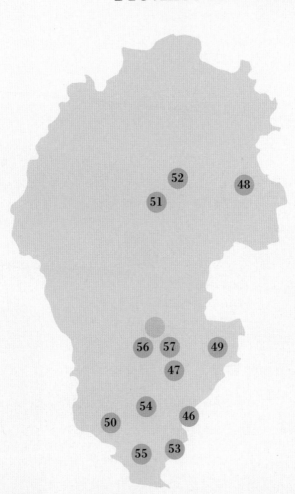

Province of Vicenza

46 – Villa Saraceno, Caldogno, Saccardo, Peruzzi, Schio, Lombardi

Agugliaro, Finale, via Finale 8

This villa was published in Palladio's treatise, and has therefore been attributed to him.

Typologically and chronologically it can be compared with Villa Gazzotti

in Bertesina, Villa Caldogno and Villa Pisani in Bagnolo (especially because of the triple arcade, which here has been rather simplified, and given a crowning tympanum). Over the centuries the building has been greatly altered, even though it has recently been restored.

Biagio Saraceno, who commissioned the building, was a member of the lesser nobility of the Vicenza area, and his family had developed quite a deal of agricultural clout in the area.

47 – Villa Franceschini, Priante, Anti Sola, Pasini, Canera di Salasco
Arcugnano, via Roma 5

The Vicenza silk producer Franceschini had Ottavio Bertotti Scamozzi (1719-1790), editor of *Le fabbriche e disegni di Andrea Palladio*, build the villa between 1770 and 1779.

The position of the villa affords an enviable panorama over the ridge of the volcanic rock plateau between the valleys of Retrone and Bacchiglione. What in Palladio's villas was usually a jutting pronaos leading into the *piano nobile* area raised on a mezzanine basement has been turned into a hexastyle loggia with Corinthian columns set against the wall with the restricted lateral intercolumniation flush against the walls for the *piano nobile* and the upper mezzanine, which are placed over an entire floor. Here there is the entrance to the villa proper, provided by a rather modest central Serliana. In the second half of the 19th century, Negrin added Romantic-style adjoining buildings, as well as garden statues, Neoclassical stuccoes in the villa itself and precious antique painting collections.

48 – Villa Rezzonico
Bassano del Grappa, Riva, via Ca' Rezzonico 60

Probably built between the 17th and 18th centuries, of uncertain authorship (some have even attributed the villa to Baldassare Longhena!), the villa follows the "Villa-Castle" scheme, set among four angular towers, but with a cornice following the line of the overhang and a simple, Baroque portal. There is a scenic central hall, with linked columns and ashlar arches,

balustrades, stuccoes and cornices, sculptures, a *Fede* (*Faith*) painted by Antonio Canova, and *Aurora* by Antonio Pellegrini, a *Notte* (*Night*) and *Carità* (*Charity*) by Busato and a large ceiling painting by Giambattista Volpato. There is also a very impressive collection of antiques.

The *barchesse in* front of the villa been given a series of ashlar Tuscan columns, the corner ones of which and those under the small central pediment are set in pairs. The *barchesse* were perhaps the work of Antonio Gaidon, from Bassano.

49 – Villa Chiericati, Da Porto, Ongarano, Rigo

Grumolo delle Abbadesse, Vancimuglio, via Nazionale 1

According to a Palladian drawing, currently in London, the project dates back to 1551, like the project for Palazzo Chiericati which dominates the square in front of the Teatro Olimpico. The commissioners for both buildings were the Chiericati brothers: Girolamo commissioned the *palazzo*; while Giovanni commissioned the villa, which was built between 1554 and 1558. The fact that there are no *barchesse* or other agricultural buildings leads to the conclusion that the villa was intended as a formal residence. The villa constitutes an important development in the evolution of Palladio's architectural language: for the first time he placed a pronaos with columns on the façade of the building, thus introducing an element that was to define the typology of the Veneto villa, both of the Palladian and Neo-Palladian types, and its future developments over the next few centuries, both in Europe and beyond. The final result, however, is so different from the original Palladian drawing, most probably because of the architect who worked on the building, that doubts have been raised as to its effective author: the Ionic pronaos is indeed impressive, but just a little excessive for the small building; the entrance steps are rather humble; and the columns devoid of entasis (a central bulge, used to give the impression that the columns are under an enormous strain from the weight of the building, taken from Greek architecture) are by no means Palladian. The internal layout has also been varied. Even though it is well-balanced, it does present one of those elements in the main prospect that have been vehemently criticised: the fireplaces in the two transversal rectangular rooms, on either side of the building, have been placed in the central area of the inside façade wall, thus forcing the architect to place the windows too close to the corners of the building. This has led to a structural weakening, and has also compromised the aesthetics of the building. This is one of the most basic "mistakes" in architecture, and even Palladio had the following to say about it in his *Quattro libri dell'architettura*: "The windows must be placed as far away as possible from the corners, or angles of the building: hence that part of the building should present no openings of any sort, for it must hold up and hold together the rest of the Building" (from Book I).

50 – Villa Pisani, De Lazara Pisani, Ferri De Lazara
Lonigo, Bagnolo, via Risaie 1

The project for the villa can be dated back to 1541-1542, and the building was complete by 1544. This is therefore the second villa that can be attributed to Palladio after Villa Godi, and is one of the first works he was commissioned when he returned from Rome in 1541, and the first for a patrician Venetian called Giovanni Pisani.

Built over the remains of a 14th century building belonging to the Vicenza nobleman Girolamo Nogarola, whose possessions were expropriated for "anti-Venetian" behaviour during the extenuating war against the Cambrai League, the villa was the first in the Renaissance to use classically-inspired temple architecture for a "lay" building. Set between two towers, the villa has been given a triple supporting arch inserted within a trabeated order holding up a triangular tympanum which was later to be developed into an entrance pronaos (Villa Chiericati, for example). This was to become the symbol *par excellence* of Palladian and Neo-Palladian architecture the world over.

The main façade overlooks the river Guà, whose banks were later built up so much that they greatly compromised the original image of the prospect. The Doric ashlar loggia recalls Porta Nuova by Michele Sanmicheli in Verona and the northern side of Palazzo Te by Giulio Romano in Mantua. The two-apsed plan is perhaps reminiscent of the Raphaelesque loggia at Villa Madama in Rome. The overall effect of Doric orders, ashlars and towers brings to mind not so much the idea of refined elegance as rustic force and earthiness.

The loggia leads to the central "T"-shaped room with cross-vault ceiling, which is a rereading of the old, Byzantine idea of a passage-hall which has always been used in Venetian buildings, but adding the idea of spaciousness typical of Roman thermal baths. Lighting is provided by a so-called "thermal" or "Palladian" window, which is the only characterising element in an otherwise simple prospect giving onto the garden.

Very few of the internal frescoes are extant.

51 – Villa Godi, Porto, Piovene, Valmarana, Malinverni

Lugo di Vicenza, Lonedo, via Andrea Palladio

On the eastern slopes of the Valdastico, the building is "placed atop a hill with a beautiful view, and alongside a river, which serves as its fish-pond. To make this site appropriate for the purposes of a Villa, courtyards have been constructed, and roads built over arches at great expense" (from *I quattro libri dell'architettura*, Book II, Chapter XV).

Villa Godi is thought to be Palladio's first villa, the project for which dates to about 1537 and the building itself to between 1540 and 1542. It seems to make use of the opposite prototype if compared to his later developments in terms of country residences. The main entrance, for example, is not jutting, nor does it make use of a trabeated pronaos; on the contrary, it is "moved back" into the building, while the two side wings are brought forward, enclosing a treble-arched loggia (which, it must be said, seems to be slightly overwhelmed by the surrounding structures). What's more, the side wings have not been developed, and the overall building gives the impression of being a severe, single block.

When Palladio published the project in his treatise more than thirty years later, he gave it a much more vertical form than the mainly horizontal and static form of the real building, which recalls Villa Trissino in Cricoli, restructured by Gian Giorgio Trissino (Palladio himself had worked on the restructuring).

The external sobriety of the building belies the rich frescoes within which Girolamo Godi commissioned Giambattista Zelotti and his workshop, Battista del Moro and Gualtiero Padovano to undertake.

The villa also houses a museum of fossils collected by Andrea Piovene, a gallery of 19th century Italian paintings, a marvellous park and a tavern.

52 – Villa Piovene, Porto, Godi
Lugo di Vicenza, Lonedo, via Andrea Palladio 51

Much controversy has surrounded the authorship of this villa. Some maintain that it is Palladio's, considering its proximity to his very first villa (Godi, Porto, Piovene, Valmarana, Malinverni). The hexastyle Ionic pronaos dates from 1587, and the side wings are characterised by their extreme simplicity. The setting is particularly beautiful, and is highlighted by the staircase that very gradually leads to the grandiose staircase of the pronaos itself. This, along with the side *barchesse* with their Doric porticoes, are by Francesco Muttoni (circa 1740), while the many statues are by Orazio Marinali. Tommaso Piovene was the first commissioner, while Count Antonio Piovene, himself an architect and the villa's 19th century owner, was responsible for the Romantic park. The San Girolamo oratory dates from 1496.

53 – Villa Barbarigo, Loredan, Rezzonico (Municipio)
Noventa Vicentina, piazza IV novembre

The villa, which was built between 1588 and 1590, has been variously attributed to Palladio and Scamozzi. The unknown architect, however, was most probably Venetian as opposed to Vicentine.

The building is extremely imposing and can be read as an arbitrary Baroque interpretation of formal Palladian principles, and the complex game of Tuscan, Ionic and paired columns (which also continue on towards the *barchesse* that surround the square) are most certainly reminiscent of Vicenza's Palazzo Chiericati. The tripartite jutting section of the central area hides a cubic nucleus, which has been "cut" horizontally by the succession of Tuscan colonnades and thrust upwards by the staircase, the superimposition of the loggias and the exaggerated, particularly extravagant and almost angular pinnacle. The interior contains frescoes by Antonio Vassillacchi, also known as "L'Aliense", and Antonio Foler.

54 – Villa Fracanzan, Dal Ferro, Orgiano, Marsilio, Piovene Porto Godi

Orgiano, via san Francesco 2

The villa has almost unanimously been attributed to Francesco Muttoni and dates from 1710. It recalls Palladian language with its high pilaster strip attic and the little pediment that sits above the composite tetrastyle pronaos. To the left there is a long portico made up of ashlar arches, while the entrance is underlined by a scenic hornbeam-lined roadway which meanders for about a kilometre. There is also a chapel, a lemon-orchard, a granary, a clock-house with an art-deco aviary, fish-ponds, a farmer's house and a garden, still extant, which was laid out like Versailles and German gardens in general.

The rooms inside the villa are a rare example of 18th century architecture. The 17th century kitchen is, however, the only example in Europe of its kind, and still contains original implements and the famous rare marble sink that Napoleon wanted for the Louvre.

55 – Villa Pojana, Miniscalchi Erizzo, Bettero, Chiarello
Pojana Maggiore, Castello, via Castello 41

Palladio was commissioned to undertake the villa before 1550 by Boni-
facio Pojana, who belonged to a Vicentine family who was faithful to the
Venetian Republic and of consolidated military traditions. It was finished in about 1563. The extant building (the owner's residence and a
farmer's house to the side) does not fully correspond to the tables in Palladio's *I quattro libri dell'architettura*, nor to the preparatory drawings.
The composed elegance of the outside aspect of the building recalls the
sobriety and austerity of military life; the interior decorations equally make
use of war-like figures and figurations, clearly out of deference to the owner.

The main prospect is dominated by a very peculiar and exquisitely Palladian element, albeit interpreted in a very concise and abstract way – a Serliana crowned by an arched lintel with five oculae between the Serliana and the upper arch. The Serliana is used so often by Palladio and in so many variations that it could almost be interpreted as his own personal signature. He originally took it from both Ancient and Renaissance Roman architecture, while the arched lintel with oculae is a Lombardesque motif introduced to Rome by Bramante, who also used it for the presbytery of Santa Maria delle Grazie in Milan and the Genazzano nymphaeum, as well as for St Peter's Basilica in Rome. There is also an extremely refined use of "eared" windows, a citation from the Tempio di Sibilla in Tivoli via Raffaello.

56 – Villa Almerico, Capra, Valmarana, also known as "La Rotonda"

Vicenza, Riviera Berica, via della Rotonda 25

Even though it was finished in about 1585 by Vincenzo Scamozzi, this villa constitutes one of the most faithful executions of an original Palladio project (probably dating back to 1566), and is the most representative in terms of Palladian typology-*cum*-model, even though it was originally commissioned by the high prelate Paolo Almerico as a city *palazzo* (which is how it was published in Palladio's *I quattro libri dell'architettura*).

The building is a synthesis of a few of the most peculiar motifs of Renaissance art – above all the practical resolution of the ideal type of building using a central plan, the symbol of perfection, which most of the greatest 15th and 16th century architects dedicated themselves to (including Brunelleschi, Francesco di Giorgio, Leonardo da Vinci, Bramante, Raffaello, Antonio da Sangallo and Peruzzi), accentuated by the rotundity of the central hall and the cupola (in fact, in *I quattro libri dell'architettura*, the cupola is much higher, thus highlighting even more its central role as centripetal element, balanced by the centrifugal element of the four Ionic pronaos). The idea for the centrality of the cupola came to Palladio because of the location of the villa, which, positioned on a "gently-sloping hill [...] from which it enjoys beautiful views on all sides" (Book II, Chapter III), dominates a series of twelve surrounding hills. The villa therefore also deals with the problem of inserting an artificial object as harmoniously as possible into its natural context, and also pays homage to the serene fusion between man and nature. But the building also gives life to another "synthesis" theorised during the Renaissance, and that is the "synthesis" or fusion of the arts: architecture, sculpture, painting, decorating the landscape. Thus we have the external statues by Lorenzo Rubini and Giambattista Albanese, the fireplaces decorated by Bartolomeo Ridolfi, the frescoes by Alessandro and Giambattista Maganza, Ludovico Dorigny and Aviani, stuccoes by Rubini, Ruggero Bascapé and Domenico Fontana and the isolated chapel attributed to Carlo Borella. All of which have been set in an English-style landscape garden.

pronaos which is, however, surmounted by a sort of attic with lesenes, a typically Baroque addition. There are innovative juttings and re-entries, exedras and ashlar arches with tympanum-like heads and a large number of statues and vases along the axes.

The villa, with its 114 rooms, is not only one of the most grandiose and elaborate of Veneto villas, but also one of the most atypical. The façade is extremely clean-cut: the central jutting area, with colossal Corinthian semi-columns, a tympanum and a festoon frieze, contains the extremely large ball room.

The ground floor is almost totally devoid of decorations, which begin

57 – Villa Bertolo, Valmarana, also known as "Ai Nani" ("The Dwarfs")

Vicenza, San Bastian, via Tiepolo 6

This is a complex made up of three buildings. In 1669, the jurist and man of letters Gian Maria Bertolo had a small *palazzo* built, probably by Antonio Muttoni, which shuts off the northern courtyard. The buildings are all rather sober, and have a central staircase which leads to a terrace surrounding the *piano nobile*, forming a socle, five rows of windows grouped together in the central area and distanced from the single-light mullioned windows (one per side), with a short crowning tympanum with acroterial statues. This is all repeated along the rear prospect.

In 1720, the property was taken over by the Valmarana family, who commissioned a second residence with seven arches on ashlar pilasters linked with a broad atrium with a portico of Tuscan columns, as well as an imposing stable with a triple nave to the south, probably by Francesco Muttoni, Antonio's son.

The name of the villa derives from the eighteen statues of dwarfs by Giovanni Battista Bendazzoli (circa 1765) which are lined up along the enclosing walls.

But the villa's real claim to fame derives from its pictorial cycles, which Tiepolo undertook in 1757 in the rooms of the little *palazzo*, while his son, Giandomenico, assisted by Gerolamo Mengozzi, also called "Il Colonna", painted the scenes in the second residence.

The two Tiepolos have managed to give life to their own distinctive characters for the frescoes in question. Giambattista has filled the little *palazzo* with heroes and Olympic divinities, while Giandomenico has given us a series of domestic scenes taken from country life (dances, gypsies, charlatans, *chinoiseries* and exotic characters in picturesque, Rococo landscapes).